PICTURES FROM AN EXHIBITION

Maureen Duffy

PICTURES FROM AN EXHIBITION

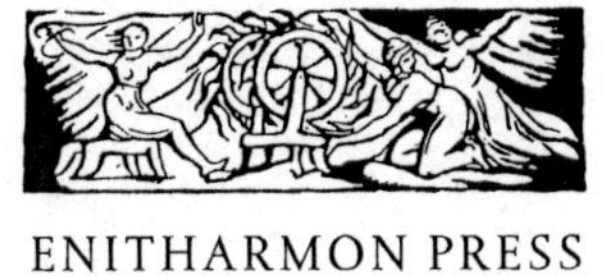

ENITHARMON PRESS

First published in 2016
by Enitharmon Press
10 Bury Place
London WC1A 2JL

www.enitharmon.co.uk

Distributed in the UK by
Central Books
99 Wallis Road
London E9 5LN

Distributed in the USA and Canada
by Independent Publishers Group
814 North Franklin Street
Chicago, IL 60610
USA
www.ipgbooks.com

ISBN: 978-1-910392-24-9

Enitharmon Press gratefully acknowledges the financial support of
Arts Council England, through Grants for the Arts.

Individuals continue to sustain the Press through the
Enitharmon Friends Scheme. We are deeply grateful to all Friends,
particularly our Patrons: Colin Beer, Duncan Forbes, Sean O'Connor and
those who wish to remain anonymous.

British Library Cataloguing-in-Publication Data.
A catalogue record for this book is available
from the British Library.

Designed in Albertina by Libanus Press
and printed in England by
Short Run Press

CONTENTS

A CHRISTMAS CONCERT

Exiles from a warmer island they practise
their art as the shoppers eddy past, one drum
upturned so the coins can ring in. Down at heel
baggy jeaned yet upright by the bus stop
with the square of boutiques and gourmet stores
their backdrop, one patters out the melody
alto and tenor, while the other bass grounds
to all the old rubbed seasonal songs
ricocheting between the twin steel skins
until feet begin to tap, smiles flit, coins skim
as we watch snow falling against the grey
city sky, shepherds astounded, magi
on their way, hear sleighbells jingle
while their small hammers tap in the tune
and only their music sings so that even
the svelte shoppers, three bags full, hesitate
pause, reach in pocket or purse, donate
their small reward for skill, in a moment
redeeming winter's, Lucy's, shortest day
and longest night, the dying god or king
with promise of returning Spring.

WILD THINGS

A flurry of black feathers huddled against
the snow, a beak lowered below the anxious
stare. Not the scourge of battlefields scavenging
for dead men's eyes or the watcher in the tower
as the heads rolled, but hesitant, debeaked
by hunger, now kin to the baby monkey
manacled in a childish game or borne
home to mother for the pot, its face
a shrivelled fear like those we sent into space
or the gazelle harried by a pride of lions.

Do we think these pictures give us sanction
for abattoir, cull, or to be just another
craftier primate, following evolution's
diktat, kill or be killed, while we admire
these images of their beauty and their pain?

OF NAMES

An old friend emails me: 'Did you know
there are five hundred others with your name
listed on the internet?' So common
in both its parts I'm not surprised. But that's
only the paternal half of the story.
Mitochondrial DNA gives quite
another, and I ask my two halves: 'How
do you fit together?' You did when
my parents' feet were set dancing in time
she seemingly a classic English
mix of Saxon and Norman; you maybe
with a dash of Viking that everyone wants
sexy-sworded, roving, not house-bound
blazoned in the fair hair, blue eyes, you
bequeathed me while hers smacked of the gypsy
dark, family legend always said we had.
So maybe on her side I can hark back
to that Asian Eve who started over
the high mountains towards the West, crossing
the plains of Europe in caravans
that would later bring pots and pans, clothes pegs
tea trays to villages whose pub windows
proclaimed: No Gypsies, though in school we sang
of the dangerous beckon of the Raggle
Taggles, and the gypsy laddie who could
spirit you away with dreams of romance
but only the cold damp ground for a bed.

Mix the two together, hers and his
wandering genes, and maybe I was
DNA doomed to rove, never to lie
easy in the goosefeather bed of habit
but dance on metred feet like those red
or hot iron shoes that never let
the wearer rest. Long before the sampling
of spit or blood, the new necromancy
could tell us our fortunes, I felt
The diddycoy pull from rocking
caravan or longboat, away from house or shore.
So are we programmed by nature and nurture
and where's that old fallacy of free will
denying the sins of the fathers that made us
monarchs or slaves by choice, not eddied to
and fro by that fate we fear now's in the blood
or tucked even snugger in our very cells?

Now we must live with this new
immortality in our flesh that maybe drives
the impulse to create though those who choose
not flesh and blood but art may never know
such human afterlife. In us our parents
die twice, unless a sibling redeems them.
Word, image, ordered sounds or facts
are all we can offer for their monument.

Nobody lived here ten thousand years ago
in a land deep frozen, scoured by glacier
and rocky moraine. Gradually we crept
back across the land bridge, still hankering

in fireside tales of Eden for the warmer
South left behind, myths we told ourselves
remembering deer, bison, lions, even
ourselves, sketched in the holy dark of caves
or figured in clay or bone, that stopped short
at what we would one day call the channel.
Then we took to the waves, became sea rovers
and maybe that's why when I was nine
a midshipman was the only life for me.

Mr Raval from Gugerat, via Uganda
greets me, taking in my dirty washing.
We exchange matters of health, the weather
his daughters' college progress. Across
the road young men from a torn island
Muslim, Hindu, Christian, bag up
my groceries. 'You alright, darling?'
they ask as the till tots up my bill.
Their ancestors went South and East
while most of mine went North and West. Now
we meet again, mingling in these streets
here in my 'pride of cities all'. My name
migrant too and shared by hundreds, meaning
the black or the dove, you can take your pick
cognate with a Scottish king and Shakespearean
victor, is only half the story, obscuring
the mother half, that North West frontier
mountain trek, outcast through Europe, lackey
to the Norman conqueror and last the native
girls: Lydia, Maisie, Minnie, Maude
Ada, Grace and Dodge, children of migrants

from country village to city smoke whose
brothers would retrace the old wheel tracks
to fight in India. Behind me in the bus
I can hear a woman's low voice, in a Slavic
tongue I can't understand. So how do I
know she is calling her lover? But I do.

ON A BEE THAT STUNG MY FINGER

I thought you were dead, that scrunched-up tangle
of wire on the kitchen tiles. But you had enough
life in you still to sting my finger, a last shot
at survival that I knew would surely kill you.
I'd picked you up instead of reaching for dustpan
and brush, in some quixotic, road-to-hell gesture
to put you out through the garden door to moulder
down to compost or be breakfast for ants, those other
stingers, and I'm sorry you're dead, knowing
every bee is precious in our pesticide times
and that we're told you flourish best now in towns
gardens, parks, joining the rest of us urbans.

And so I relish my 'bee-loud' rambler
and funnelling foxglove mouths you make soft
sound boxes for the whirr of your wings but
as I draw your small, black dart from my flesh
I curse out loud, 'You ungrateful bugger!'
though knowing I would do the same in my own
way: 'This animal defends itself if attacked.'

So now I know you're really dead I pick you
up again. Your wings have spread in death proclaiming
you aerial, and I flick you out through the door
to join your mates browsing the wild blue
campanula, sweet foraging above the small
black, furry body, the translucent wings.

'OH DON'T YOU HEAR THE TURTLE DOVE…?'

No turtles for us, beloved, in this time
of the singing of birds. Someone snared
the last one winging our way from Africa
so no 'lamenting for its own true love'
in our branches though 'I will mourn for thee'
sickness has laid low as those whose lovers
were all at sea sending their sorrows back
ten thousand miles, lamented alone.

Still, I solace myself with another fable
the one that has the amorous turtle
and fiery phoenix as loving mates
culling comfort from their legend of hope
that we too will take wing again and rise
out of the ashes of this bleak Spring.

MARRAKESH

The palm leaves tremble in a draft I can't feel
viridian plumage that would loft the scaly
trunk, green shuttlecock, skywards, yet sparrows
hop in the sandy grass and blackbirds chortle
from the hotel cliff-tops while the tarmac
seethes outside under forty degrees.

I stole this paper from the receptionists' desk
to tell how today we were bussed out of
our tourist palaces where we're pooled, cossetted
to visit the old city, medina, souk of broken
bikeways where the desperate huckster carpets
woven by Berber women in the desert heights
and potions, while a woman squats on the dusty
tiles, ceaselessly grinding herbs in a hand quern
round and round as we watch, jewels and pots, so we
can carry home a bit of the place, 'your souvenir'.

But I want to take home the thin cat couched
languidly against the angle of an alleyway
rose sand coated like the desert beyond the walls
who looked up at me, questioning. I speak
to her. Then, when I turn to go, she gets up
to follow and something in my heart breaks
as I tell her: 'You can't come with me. Go back.'

NATURAL HISTORY

They thought they were true all those stories
of randy unicorns, bloody breast feeding
pelicans, ambergris breathing whales, they
who were us back then. Now we watch on screen
our surrogates, elsewhere, where we may
never go, marvelling at their lives, loves, deaths
drawing the same morals from the tales:
how the kudu, gashed, bloodied in the fight
for a mate, brought to his knees is prey
to leopards, or how the kingfisher pesters
his love with minnows, while others dance
and display, eye-catching with ruffs, or fantails
dandy as any knee-britched count or courtier.

But my favoured fable can't be shown
or told. We are still fashioning it.

STORM

How you would have hated this storm, the lightning dash
and bomb-blast of thunder, and I would have hurried
home from school so you shouldn't be alone
to find you crouched behind a door, in a corner
under the stairs. And it wasn't a memory
of the latest thunderclap that had sent you
scuttling, not the one that buried us both
but that childhood strike of a bolt against
your 1890s' workhouse style high brick
Board School when you fled over the wall
to Granny's and were marked missing at roll-call
whose centenary I commemorate here
of never-to-be-forgotten terror for you
who were so brave every winter in the face
of that death that finally ran you down, when
every stifled cough might throw up your life's blood.

And when the real bomb fell whispered to our
rescuers: 'Take my little girl out first.'

Superstitious about images I cling on
to old snapshots of long dead dogs and cats
afraid to kill a second time shapes that still
run and jump, demand and give in memory
to erase them forever as though
in the old saw of terror 'they had never been'.
And as for the living how can I tempt fate
with fire or scissors, and so the drawer fills up.

Yet they're not us, these faces, masks, muzzles
that stare from celluloid or screen. And this latest
put into my hand by a still sad widow
of five years, shows a group of us I can
number my dead among, memorial
to a buried decade, gone yet visible
in this shiny icon. But these stills can't show
how they ran through fields, laughed or were lovers.
Memory has to fit them up with life again
though still I turn them over hoping to catch
their voices, friends of fur or flesh, part of
my story I retell again and again.

FOR ART'S SAKE

'Je voudrais seulement être aimée et aimer.'
JANE AVRIL

Waif dancing, mask white, as ladies once leaded
their cheeks, legs akimbo or baby doll
skirt bunched over the bloomers
to give a hint of leg, a Shirley Temple
frisson to all her sugar daddies.

'Born in a brothel, bastard survivor
I let them believe legging it cured me
of holy madness, or the tarantella
from the sting of a maternal slap.

And the little guy always sketching me
from the corner, his legs cut down while my
skinny shanks boleroed wildly, he made me
famous, waiting at the stage door when
I left, eyes cast down, gone inside myself
freed from those other eyes that had held me
spinning their desires or lusting till I began.

I became a whirling dervish, a knees-up
bacchante while he hatched, etched
set me for all time in stone. The rest
of my life an afterword, encore of lovers
sickness, two world wars, a lost child
charity, memorials. And the little man
with the half-mast shins? He died long ago.

But I am still here, ludic on these walls
in his lines and dashes, my mask in place
a leaf twirling for their delectation
and mine, until, the music over, at ease
hair aflame, among my top-hatted
punters with faces like Breughel painted
tormenting Christ, my patrons who wrote
my score, setting me high-kicking while
the windmill bloodily ground in a new age.'

HALLOWEEN

For Karen, Stephen, Naomi and Ben

The Summit trees are decked in dying dress
maple, oak and beech flag up the summer's end
while children dance for the dead and for
a father's birth. Last night in the hotel bar
the class of '63 partied remembering
their green Spring. A red-eyed skeleton
winks at us in the cellar dining room
while gossamer fake cobwebs festoon
pictures, hedges, its plastic bones.

Do we honour the dead or mock them
with our store-bought trumpery to keep
our ghosts at bay, the grinning pumpkin skulls
whose carved eye-sockets flicker as if
they fluttered their lids inviting us
to some grand conspiracy that dead
isn't really dead but keeps a malevolent
eye on the poignant doings of the living?

So at the year's turning we light bonfires
sparklers sizzle on the dark while rockets
hoist our hopes skywards before winter
shuts us in, presaging all our long nights.
But today you will be celebrating not
the envious dead but the living, rebirth
and lighting a beacon against all our winters.

MEMORIAL

Sandham Chapel

Now, seeing these scenes again, after sixty years
a war away, of another war, I still marvel
how you transfigure bloody bed spreads into
holy vestments, sheets become angel wings
tea urns sacred grails, how broken bodies
or merely banal tasks coalesce into
pietas you saw once on older frescoed walls
and never forgot even in the din
of that war we remember this year but
can't celebrate. Wasn't it the war
to end all wars with homes fit for heroes
homecoming? Instead Depression, the dole queue
and then more marching boots, arms upraised
in a new salute entrenching hatred.

The men you drew from memory are all
dead meat now though they live on your walls still
not knee deep in mud but washing, nursing
their wounds or in the relief of sleep as if
slumped snoring against a sarcophagus.

You showed only war's respites for those who'd
'copped a Blighty one', or out of battle
now their crosses laid aside, brushing
away the earth, they amble towards armistice
daybreak at the top of the hill. The horses
ears pricked, shoulder off the dirt, stagger

to their feet, waiting for orders, not knowing
the butchery to come, while the figures above
on the hill, shrunk by distance, receding
as Piero taught, into matchstick men, go on
their way into our deluding dawn.

SNAPSHOT

Sorting through the old snaps I'd brought you
you remembered perfectly the stout woman
squatting beside the breakwater, stockinged legs
flung out on the sand: 'Mrs Permain!' you said
effortlessly reaching back seventy years to when
I was too young to remember. This was
our childhood, you seven years older, and now
I bring you these blurred records you love, our
past, turning them over, holding them close
for scrutiny: 'Oh yes, that's Nellie next door.'
Yet you can't recall what I said minutes
ago. Does it matter? You are so happy
in our game of remembrance. 'Bring me
some more,' you say, 'next time you come.'
And I will. Oh I will, before that light is snuffed out.

CRAIGLOCKHART

For Acting Company Sergeant Major J F Williamson

Their boots brought back the spores that a century
later unfurl in these pale tendrils, those that could
hardly put one foot before the other so clogged
muddied, muddled with all they'd tramped through.
'Shell shock' they called it. Just too much of din
death, corruption, the desolation of No man's
land with its tapestry of wire-hung corpses.

I remember a story you told me of the
'windy' boy who was too scared to stand
on the trench's fire-step crying: 'I know
I'm going to die,' and how you talked to him
in that calm voice I also remember, but never
told me how he fared, whether he came back
as you did. Still it would have been worse
to be shot for cowardice than going
over the top. You weren't one of those
invalided to Craiglockhart like the soldier
poets. You, as they say: 'soldiered on', and anyway
it was only for officers. I know you would
have understood why it had become too much
for them because once you told me: 'I'm dead
too, like them back there'. And you'd have seen
the irony in these filaments, bean shoots
of fungus still sprouting where the boots trod

pushing their bone-white fronds up into the air
in the hospital grounds where skilled medics
cultivated verses out of their patients' pain
that can still uncurl livid fronds in our
latterday hearts. Then sent them back to die.

The roof's a double upturned hull as if shipwrecked
against platform reefs; old brick for sides with eyehole
roundels pierced to let the smoke out, sky in, to this beached
Titanic whose iron ribs are fretted with circles
and stars while their mainstays rest on fluted heads
and heraldic town crests fill the armpits of classic
gothic pillars in civic pride. Here trains first began
to run, bringing coals to Newcastle, then webbing out
criss-crossing the globe with human cargo.

Now their sleek descendant ferries me South.
But waiting on the platform a memory
sidles back, a real remembering or some
fiction I've told myself, of the old works
where tired engines came to be made new
their clinkered boilers stacked with fresh guts
a long-ago exhibition to celebrate what
I can't recall, only the clangour, the smoke
and looking up, up on a high rail
the old 'Coffee Pot' chuffing like a toy
train, tall chimneyed, its stove-pipe hat
held high, the grind of pistons, metal on
metal, boiler's stamp and hiss, bygone now
as Stevenson's first *Locomotion*
or Cook's *Endeavour*, its masts rocked
by the Tees in a convoy of swans, last
safe berth, home from Australia.

EVIE EXILED

I never knew you well though we were neighbours
for thirty years. We took in parcels for each other
exchanged Christmas cards: 'Evie and Family.'
'Auguri. Buon Anno!' Sometimes a glass of wine.
Now your blowsy camellias are in full spate
again, blooms as big as saucers, like the last
dog's eyes in The Tinder Box, florid in cerise
damask, the colour too of those you brought
from home, under drowsy Italian twilights
strolling arm in arm down village streets
Bella di Notte, Beauty of Night in English
that you planted in the square of earth where a slim
tree sprang out of our urban pavement
in front of your house you couldn't leave, except
in your daughter's car on hospital trips
though I would see you still in the garden
or on the terrace tending your loved plants.

Now your camellia's house high and I wait
for the incomers who will move in and fell it
to make way for fashion's latest extension
not knowing how it must have reminded you
in your own tongue of long lost Lucca.
You never quite mastered English, preferring
a marriage of the two and glad to find
I understood. So you once confessed how
all those post-war years ago, you'd never
wanted to marry the chosen husband. You
wanted to be a teacher, not to come to

this cold island and be wedded to a
trattoria beside the Thames. And that
you'd admired Il Duce because he made
the trains run on time with Northern precision
and you found my mezzogiorno drawl too sloppy
lacking Firenze's staccato perfection.

Soon the builders will move in, roofing over
your oleander terrace, gobbling up
the garden for a conservatory.
And the day the tallest camellia falls I shall
hear your voice scolding, con brio, as the last
plush petals sink to the ground.

HIGH RENAISSANCE
After Veronese

'We take the same freedom as poets and jesters,'
the painter told the Inquisition when summoned
before them for crowding out Christ and his mates
where they sat at supper, with jesters, dwarfs
drunken Germans, 'scurrilities, heresy'.
They made him change the title to one where gospel
said 'He sat with sinners in the House of Levi'.

Such abundance: 'If I see a space I fill it
with a figure.' Always a dog or two, monkey
or creamy ermine. In other scenes horses'
noble heads and hair you could plait, an ox
and ass of course, nature always present
among the lush limbs, the sumptuous jewels
a skim of milky veil or stomacher in warp
and weave laid on so true you can feel
the ridged cloth. But above all the girls
Lucrezia, Helena, Magdalene
heads in their hands or half turned away
so natural we can read their faces, their pain.
Except for Judith who turns her head in disgust
unwilling to look at the bloody severed thing
as she drops it into the maid's satchel.

And then the lavish white flesh of Venus
just to show he could do that too. Nothing
was out of bounds with the same freedom
'of poets and jesters'. So now I take it back
that same licence to celebrate again
a full, remembered breast, your contoured back.

Did she struggle that Iphigenia
or, as some say, go quietly, offering
her bare virgin breasts to the knife's prick
that let out her heart's blood and let the warriors'
ships sail on? Or, as others have it
did Artemis take pity on her and snatch
her up from the stony altar, leaving
a hind to suffer in her stead, as the girls
of Troy would do, raped, enslaved, their children
butchered before their eyes, spitted on spear or sword.

Oh those were barbarous times and it couldn't
happen now. So what are those most bitter
fruit the banyan trees bear, and why didn't
Lakshmi descend with a couple of nanny goats
and bear away her daughters? But maybe
it was for the best. No man wants tainted meat
as Clare wrote in another time, another place.
Except for Helen carried home to happy
ever after but then she was the daughter
of gods, not common mortals or even
heroes. So she could run off with her young
lover, maybe just to show unkind man
she was no one's property. Afterwards
of course they claimed she'd been kidnapped.

And maybe it was all just an excuse
for another trade war, for power, markets
empire. But still it goes on. Two hundred
who just wanted to learn like their brothers
reft away from their desks into the forest
over the border. And if they are ever
tracked down will they too be unwanted flesh
to live out their days dependent for a roof
a meal, on sisters-in-law, mothers
despised by the whispering tongues?

'What were you wearing?' the judge asks the victim
'and was there a previous relationship?'
meaning: did you give some signal, tempt
your fate? And as for those trafficked
into slavery, seeking asylum, we'll send
you back to where you're not wanted as
soiled goods, no happy Helenic homecoming for you.

The bitter fruit of the banyan hang still
as death while Iphigenia in Tauris
priestess of Artemis, as another
of her girls, rescues her brother from
sacrifice so all's well that ends well.
She did as she was told, lay down on the cold

altar like a good little girl. But the fate
of those fruit of the banyan tree we can't know
whether they pleaded, wept as one after
another took them, knowing they could never
go home to fathers and brothers they had
dishonoured, to be stoned for adultery
or turned away to sell themselves on the streets
while we paper over the truth with myth
and Iphigenia lights the altar flame
whose smoke hides her true fate. The women
of Troy, Nigeria, Ruanda, the girls
of Gujarat and Brixton are still
sisters, in and out of their skin.

The red and green pygmy grenades of the crab pear
ricochet off the roadway or bombard the roof
and bonnet of the white van parked below.
'You can make jelly out of them,' Denny
from down the road tells me but no one
harvests them, gathers them up. They're corralled
shovelled into the street cleaner's wheeled cart
to become landfill where at least they'll rot down
to compost, unlike most of our leavings.

So should we chop them down? Don't they just
tangle up the telephone wires, run their roots
into our basements, stain the autumn pavements
with their squeezed pith and bitter perry?

But in Spring, after winter's murk, they put on
their white bridals and marry the street.

BLACK ON BLACK
For Anselm Kiefer

Growing up in the aftermath your colours
are grey and black, the tones of grief and guilt
with only a sprinkle of stardust hinting
at hope. You, we, are alone in the blasted
or frozen landscapes of nightmare, where
even the sunflowers are burned black.
Only the artist's palette wings up while
you articulate the burden of history
in memorial towers of ashen canvasses
or steely heaps of books too heavy
to lift the heart on outspread leaden wings.
Exalted empty chairs are the trinity's
vacant thrones. The godhead has gone to join
Odin and Thor now Solomon's love song
resounds through a vaulted oven.

Born a war before you I still remember
the heaped bones strung together with shrivelled
sinew, humanoid with only an echo
of flesh and blood, a boney semblance:
the Belsen dolls. And our own grey guilt
that we didn't see until too late. The poets'
words stumble among the parched furrows:
Celan, Wilde, Woolf exhaling the only
human breath, except for your lone figure
upright or stretched out, corpsed, sprouting
a tree of life from your guts, as we try
to do, flailing against history, manstory
prestory, before there was anyone

to tell it in song or paint or rhymes:
Pleistocine, Cambrian, Devonian
the labels we tack on to try to pin down
aeons before us while we trawl our nets
to catch the recent past, mystory
then yours by adoption; black on black.

You set love against it, innocent boy
bodies, soft and white to negate cold steel
lead, ash. Yet the way out leads through
the Black Forest again as we leave
recalling another war, the blasted
stumps of Nomansland, its ashen earth.

LAST LIGHT

Everything had to be light, was light.
Even solid shapes were echoes of themselves
ephemera, ghost glimpses through curtains
of light motes falling on gully, city
shadow ships, as he 'took wing' or rather
stumped South where light was pure, leaving behind
the smudged skies from mill, forge, grate, sketchbook
in hand, chronicling the lands he passed through
as insubstantial as dreams, then home again
remembering, poured the milky light over
paper and canvas till it shone afresh.

Nothing could hold him still except brush
palette, pigment. He was capturing the minute
so if his visions would fade, the colours dim
that was the nature of things. Like the river
at Mrs Booth's Cheyne Walk door he saw all things
in flux; the new locomotive speeding into
its own steam cocoon, the whalers' stove pipes
sullying the sky with their sooty breath
above the bloodied waters, morning's mist
in evening shimmer, for what can we know
capture, hold, only a touch here and there
of richer colour, a moment caught
a trick of the light?

The dark spread from inside: an abandoned
child, of a mother dying in Bedlam
a younger sister at four. Only art
and light to ease an eleven year old's
exile. So he set out every summer
searching for where it fell pure in rays
fine as sea spray from peak, lake and mast
to catch it again in winter with paper
and paint, the butcher's grandson, wig maker's
child who'd made it good, friend to the nobility
portraying their summer palaces, sleeping
in their beds, distrusting the love of women
tetchy, proud, chasing the black dog with
bribes of money and fame yet still it snarled and whined.

But there was always Margate where the air
was salt pure and gleaming, away from smog
humanity's press and fever in shuttered
rooms, and those final evocations
the fleet setting sail for the last time
with tears and hands waving. And then white
on white, unfinished or maybe just a luminary
shower soaking the scene, the thin yet
tactile wash of ivory, vanilla, cream.

PLAYING OUT; PLAYING IN

We played out round the lamp-posts under
their yellowy light when we were kids
till twilight when the mothers called: 'Home time!'
from the doorsteps or sometimes a child's name:
'Mar-i-lyn!' echoing through the dusky streets.
Then we unslung the rope we'd played
Tarzan on from the lamp-posts' outstretched arm
gathered up our marbles from the gutter
pocketted our conkers, went home to tea
in winter, bed in long summer evenings.

We were warned of course never to speak
to strangers or take their proffered sweets
so when the Yankee doughboys held out
silver coins, money to go with them into the park's
screening bushes we knew to say no
and to 'stick together', with 'safety in numbers'.

So there's nothing new under the sun except
that now you're alone in your bedroom with
none of the gang to run off with, laughing
and catch the swinging rope, knowing you're
Tarzan, invincible among your jungle
mates, and the streets your safe playground
as long as you followed the rules.
Those days playing out into the dusk
taught us invention, resilience.

Now it's the one you don't know, can't see
only the enticing avatar who says he's just a kid
like you or maybe he wants to treat you
thinks you're beautiful, clever, and can you
meet but best not to tell the grown-ups
'our secret'. So playing in is full of hazards
deceit, betrayal, with fear of the streets
beyond given over now to car, van, bus.
'Send me your picture,' the message says
'here's mine. Meet me,' where there are no mates
to run laughing away with as you dangle
from the rope of words and Mum doesn't
know when to call: 'Home time! Mar-i-lyn!'

PHILAE'S SONG

They called me after the end of the old world
where Egypt fell into the sea, for wasn't I
meant to go to their longed-for nemesis
that spinning block of ice and rock they thought
would tell them how they began, those clever apes
who fashioned me and gave me to Rosie, my
foster mother, to carry to the edge
of their universe where the starlight shines cold
away from the warm arms of my mother
and theirs, Gaia. Spindly, an unclothed bedstead
sibling to those probes they send dealing death
I bounced on my trestle shanks in the thin
force that couldn't hold me, so different
from mother earth's hug close to her
though I'd almost forgotten its strength
as we reeled through time and space, on and on
until Rosie hung over the spot where she
must let me drop. And so I went. I am
the end, and almost the end of their hopes
three times before I could settle and give them
what they wished, had made me for, their end.

I wasn't just named for an ending. There was
a temple to rebirth, to Isis, healer, creator
of new life and I am meant to give them
wisdom, light as I nestle into this new world
and begin my song. In time I might become
native, calcify into my rocky bed unless
they can call me back, I earn my passage home.
So what shall I tell them? That its forefathers

pocked their planet with life giving elements?
I lean on my cold rock, one foot in air
under the cliff's deep shadow as my life blood
drains away with no sunlight to rekindle it.
But I do my job, send them pictures, even
drill down, risking a final fall into the abyss
that waits below the sheer cliff wall.

I am falling asleep but I told them almost
all I know before the blinds came down
tweeted it to dear Rosie hovering
above me. She won't leave me here alone
on my bare bed. Although she can't hear me
any more, we'll go on together towards
their star while she circles my resting place
until one day maybe I can sing again
when the sun warms my glass veins
wakens me from my long sleep, their avatar
to tell them they too are just stardust
that will turn to ash as the sun dwarfs
into darkness, sucking us down into
oblivion or new worlds and I sing my
swansong. Unless they relent, bring me home
riding on Rosie's shoulders, a flying angel
to languish, museum-bound, among
the skeletal dinosaurs, fragments
of meteorite, the first space suit.
And children will ask: 'What was Philae?
What did it do among the wheeling stars?'

INTERIORS

Leonardo had to wait till the subject
was dead to see past skin and muscle
to bone. Now we can peer straight through.
So I examine the ghostly image
of my mouldered hip joint, the vertebrae
that still keep me more or less upright.
Such interiors furnish our mortality.
Not the tinkling spinet we can almost hear
from Vermeer, plucking our heartstrings
with promise of order, bourgeois comfort
that will coda on happy ever after
and a painter's supple brush to record
it all as we stand before it now, admiring
the muted tones, the enduring tranquillity.

Except that the girl is reading a letter
and the weevil, blindworm desire munches
at the edges, lurks in the shadows
and in the mirror behind the woman
the painter's face, as in Narcissus' pool, floats.
They were no different then: the calm and order
careful stroking sable, couldn't gloss over
the everyday of desire and loss, lodged
in the bone, muscle, under the skin
carried in the chemistry of the coursing blood.

And that vital organ the heart is not just
a mere pump, but an icon we still make for our love.

IN THE NATIONAL GALLERY, EDINBURGH

Here in this city I admire but do not know
to love, with above and beyond, Scott's spire
piecing an oyster canopy of sky while below
lies the green gorge where they used to dump
detritus, bodies, all the human waste
that gave the city its nickname: 'auld reekie'
fringed now by the glossy fronts of Princes Street
with logos familiar from every city
centre where we've driven out the butcher
the baker, the candlestick maker, I watch
the gulls rooting in the sward while a lone crow
stalks the garden paths. Once I could get lost
in his high romance. I was Ivanhoe
and when we sang in assembly of knights
in the stories of old I saw myself riding out
and can still mount my ricketty nag
and lift my rusty sword against dragons
though they're not the laily worm it was easy
to behead with a single blow but a many
headed hydra or Behemoths as they harry
the land sucking all into their devouring maw.

So I turn instead looking for consolation
to pictures in an enduring exhibition
and find you here, my talisman, Venus
with her boy Cupid, a teenage mother
and her impish son, and my alter ego
Actaeon, horned by Diana's girls, and torn
by his own desires. Rubens' lush ladies
I recognise at once across their gilded room.

But there's no time to catch Anadyomene
wringing the birth foam from a plaited tress
no Botticelli slip of a girl under Titian's brush
it's hard to believe her soft flesh has risen
new born from the labouring waves that now
caress her breakwater thighs while a fragile
scallop shell, too small to have been her cradle
drifts away on the tide. A brahmah of a woman
she would have been called in my childhood
when no catwalk waif got a place in the
chorus line, and slim signified a greensick
girl who would die before being a bride.

And now I am travelling South through the art
of song where collier and weaver once sang
of love and lock-out, hunger and pit death
past abandoned slagheaps grassed over and
boarded-up mills and factories, stilled wind
and water wheels. 'Poetry makes nothing
happen,' one poet said, remembering
another who had tried for change. But against
that I set the striking minstrel miners
begging bowls, Piers ploughing his half acre
in cadenced lines that fed a revolution
and art, paint and form that quickens breath
and heartbeat as the pictures step down
from their frames to walk among us.

Still life against the black ground of the flat
kitchen roof, like something after Oudry
but, seen from above, cruciform with outspread
wings, and headless as if dropped from hawk
or eagle talons. How otherwise could it
get there beyond the scaling
of marauding cat or fox?

Just a few muddied yet still downy feathers
on the ground below should have hinted
at that small tragedy acted out close by.
And I can't give it decent burial as
I did the last one, done to death behind
the dustbin, under a leaf shroud, beneath
the white rambler in my urban plot.
Up there its sad shape splat on the roof
will be whittled by wind and rain until
the last breeze powders away the thin bones
the feathers fly off, and the roof canvas
is blank again, unless the cruel beaked crow
should come, glutting on your poor carrion
his crop become your devouring grave.

Oh even this small death deserves an
epitaph, and no light should go out unmourned.

DARKLING

Your portraits show you full-lipped, always
in thought, looking beyond, chin on fist
a carelessly undone cuff, epitome
of the romantic poet, an image
your friends passed down, rejecting your physician's
trade, as you never quite did but let it seep
into the poems, with an eye for the small
precisions: a limping hare, a cloud
of gnats, your garden birds.

It's seventy years, all but one, since I last
wrote to you, aged thirteen, still in white
ankle socks, school serge tunic, white blouse
still imitating your style of over
a century ago, a voice I loved
but had to let go to find my own.
This morning reading about you brought it
all back, how I fell for your faery
half Titania, half Morgan Le Fay
both witching and a riddle no one
has ever solved: whether she was poetry
passion or the all consuming death
that took your mother, and mine, in our
early teens, its starved lips and pale cheeks.

Our lives seemed so similar I expected
to die like you, and three of my aunts
in my twenties, but you led me into
poetry, lamenting your death, and in thrall
to your life but only knowing the last lone

star you sang of with your dying breath
and never understanding till now how
you could know in the flickering candlelight
that bright drop on the sheet was your death knell.

Now I see it all in you walking the wards
'alleviating' you called it, with the calm
skill that could take a pistol ball from a woman's
neck and save her life, then hold it up in
the witness box, evidence against her
would-be killer. There you'd heard 'men hear
each other groan', seen the daily tally
of crushed limbs, poisoned flesh, 'spectre
thin youth' that haunt your lines as you tried
to bandage our wounds with beauty while
sawbones fitted peglegs to Waterloo stumps.

And at last your first published poem in May
heralding a summer where the 'murmurous
flies' drank dewy wine at the muskrose cup
freeing you from those corridors of pain.
But then your first collection, that rite
of passage for every poet earned
only contempt for the cockney upstart.
So you thought you would put to sea as
ship's surgeon but you were called home
from tramping the Scottish hills to nurse
your brother Tom and who better than
the doctor in the family, only
to fall in love with the girl next door

'a passion that killed you' as a jealous
friend described it. Her mother forbad
marriage to the starveling poet. Parted
already ill, your faery forbidden
you wrote and wrote, letters, poems till
the last desperate trip to Rome crying:
'I should have lived and I should have had her.'

I follow your beautiful script across
the pages that are your true portrait
laying bare your delicate lineaments.
Severn lifted you up in his arms as you
choked on your own blood as my mother's
welled up staining the pavement. But the words
the words run on, the 'teeming brain' was gleaned
shimmering down the years so that so long
after they were still a talisman
touchstone and my bright leading star.

FLESH

The dwarf peers over the lady's shoulder
while Fido scrabbles at her skirt. She's dreaming
with an almost smile on her lips, of another life
than that of the ornate chair that enthrones
her, richly robed, of the naked flesh it enfolds.
Under his brush flesh sang, throbbed with the
coursing blood. These living limbs beckon from
their frames while others grow faint, pale
into mere painted images beside them.
And the faces too look out of his canvas
down through the centuries, still saying
'I am you though I lived in this shuttered room
and walked the streets of Antwerp more than
three hundred years ago'. He feared the dark
side, the brutish lust that lurks behind Venus
while she recoils from such swart desire
unleavened by love; a whimpering cupid
cowers at her feet; her lower lip trembles
with fear or disgust, goddess yet woman too.

And when the courtier asked if he was
a diplomat who amused himself
with painting he answered: 'I am a painter
who amuses himself as a diplomat'.
So he shuttled between countries seeking
peace, honoured, knighted, the 'prince of painters'
Spain, England, France and back to Antwerp.
There were eight mouths to feed at home
studio toilers to pay, paint, brushes, canvas
frames to buy, models, though it was better

to marry your Venus, first Isabella
then teenage Helene, her niece, fifty years
his junior, Pan to her Syrinx. The canvases
unrolled: mythologies, altar pieces, portraits
or sometimes just his own child's face looked out
or the whole family posed in Sunday best.

Then at the last, retired to his country estate
a new art of landscape, serene after
the dervish dance of limbs, colour, forms
that would quicken those of others centuries
after. Yet most, gazing at Helene's sweet
flesh, he reminds me how I have lain close
to your living breasts, the remembered
loving that held back time.

BURDSONG

BURDSONG

1.

Cold rain sluices the pavements. My city
knows I'm leching after faraway.
She lowers over me, complaining
of neglect, of love withdrawn from my
London become an alien land, now
my heart's home's elsewhere, where you are.

2.

Once you have called the day's a slattern
I have to chivvy through laggard hours
of drudging tasks. But today the sun's
come out. You will be walking from the station
head up, arm swinging, while I stand
at the window, watching, waiting.

3.

In bed we're the same height only my arms
are longer to reach around your shoulders
where I can plant kisses, to smooth your
smoother breast. So it doesn't matter
about leg length, mine still sinuates easy
between yours as we lie equal, face
to face making love instead of dreams.

4.

Kisses are my comfort food I could
glut on and never be sated. But time
and tides ration our lips meeting
as if afraid we might tire of browsing
our land of milk and honey.

5.

Old Galen was wrong then with his
'triste omne animal'. We laugh, kiss
make tea, cling together against
parting. But read on. Didn't he add
something about women and cock
a doodles being different? Like
the pigeons on the window-sill
who burble their own longing song
while we lie loving. As if they knew.

6.

Had they learned it from us, peering in
through the window, the pigeons I saw
flying vermin by popular vote
beak to beak, kissing? I know grebe dance
cormorants twine their necks in courtship
but kissing? So maybe they can learn
or we can as they coo and bill, that all
share a common litany of loving.

7.

Arm in arm together ahead of me
(is it her arm through his or his through hers?
No matter) I follow behind along
the underground platform watching to see
whether, from time to time, like us one takes
a little hop or skip, shuffle or two step
to get in harmony again. And they do.

8.

That old rogue John Dee, Elizabeth's magus
marked down each time he made love to his wife
knowing such days are propitious. So
should I mark with a kiss those times
that bring us grace and joy, these omens
from our necromancy of love?

9.

Garrulous with love I batter your ears
with endearments, old time-worn honeyed
words every lover has lavished on the
beloved since romantic love was first
born as they tell us. But I mean them.

10.

We were a long time evolving out of Eden
so why were we foolish enough to follow
our smaller brained forerunners: Australopithecus,
Erectus, Habilis, Neanderthalensis
and those lost others we haven't named yet
leaving the warm savannahs for the bleak unknown
our hill gated garden suburb where we embedded
our footprints beside the great lake, heading North
into the ice age? Yet we've never quite forgotten
search for its contours in holiday brochures
and fables of Nirvana, Utopia, Dreamland.
Strange then, or is it, that I should find it here
in this bed where we lie entwined
looking love into each others' eyes.

11.

My blackbird thinks he's a nightingale
singing into the four o'clock dark
as if it was already dawn and the chorus
in full throat. Maybe he can see from
up where, the first pale blur that I can't
or hear another singing his territory
from down the road among the graves
that my cloth ears can't catch. But into my dark
he sets spinning his carousel of notes
while I, like Sappho lie in my bed alone
with the stars veiled behind city cloud
rhyming out my longing for you.

12.

Not wanting to wash you off my skin yet
I eschew the bath, opting for what used
to be called 'a good wash up and down'
hoping a touch of your sweet balm might linger
in the folds and creases of where we lay
so close our bodies breathed, melted
into each other until I couldn't tell
anymore where you ended, I began.

13.

Today we sat like other lovers
in the park, on a bench, my arm
around you while the world went by.
Someone asked us the way to
somewhere, and then we walked on
arm-in-arm, past palaces, lost tourists
under old branches over mottled
grass, towards parting. But for a time
it was all ours, and summer.

14.

As if there were no tomorrow
because tomorrow never comes
let's, love, linger in our eternal
present laced in each other's arms
until tomorrow and tomorrow
and tomorrow brings on our dear
time's cease in parting.

15.

This second Spring in Fall rekindles
daisy and rose, weigela, kerria
even the primrose, conned by climate's change
while penstemmons still open their summer
lips to plundering bees under September's
last late warmth, whispering: 'Renew your Spring
before October dark draws down the blinds.'

16.

Tonight the clocks go back to winter time.
I'd put them back to yesterday when we
held time still while it ran on outside, beyond
the window in cloud scud, on bird wing.
Now I replay the sweet video through
my daydreams, until that time come when we can
stop the hours' gush again, holding forever
safe in each others' arms if only for that while.

17.

The dwarf iris on my window-sill bought
for a song has suddenly opened
its deep sapphire mouth telling me there will be
Spring again with its flowering of grace and joy
on lips and hands as we reawaken too.

18.

Those two pigeons on the coping
lovey-doveying beak to beak
don't know it's St Valentine's Day
when tradition says they should mate.
Maybe they're the two, perched on our
window-sill and peering in, who saw
us kissing and thought they would
give it a try. So today they're our
surrogates, standing in for us
as I watch them till the time when
we can be lip to lip again
as they murmur approval
watching us from the window-sill.

19.

Through the kitchen window I can see
though not hear, the small gnats' band
watch their dance on the gentle eddies
while the first swift mews above the man-made
cliffs of tower blocks, the gnats nemesis
if they let themselves drift up too high
and the song's 'first white butterfly' is
boozing on nectar in the weigela.
So it's Spring again 'wherein everything
renews save only...' And I wait for
our Spring's return, to break into bud
and leaf when I can hold you
in my longing arms again.

20.

After the last affirming kiss we turn away
you going yours, I mine, except that
as you go we turn to wave and then
again, until we're swallowed by
the crowds or my fears. And this small
death we trust to resurrection
believing and letting go.

NOTES

Page 7: Buskers on King's Road, Chelsea.

Page 14: The first line is that of a folksong, a widowed dove's lament.

Page 17: My mother, the 'you' of the poem, suffered a lifelong trauma about storms from her London elementary school being struck by lightning.

Page 18: 'The Camera Cannot Lie'. Yes it can and does!

Page 19: From the many paintings of her by Toulouse-Lautrec.

Page 21: My first experience of the fall and Halloween in North America, which also celebrated a father's birthday.

Page 22: Stanley Spencer's stunning canvasses from Sandham Memorial Chapel were shown at Somerset House in London in 2013–14 while the chapel at Burghclere in Hampshire was being renovated.

Page 25: A news item about the appearance of a non-native fungus in the grounds of Craiglockhart, a psychiatric hospital in Edinburgh for officers during the First World War, sparked thoughts on war trauma and class.

Page 30: Homage to Paolo Veronese, one of my favourite painters.

Page 32: The Greek ships were becalmed on their way to Troy until Agamemnon sacrificed his daughter Iphigenia, here a prototype for the sacrifices of women through rape, abduction, mental and physical violence.

Page 38: First published in *Poem* magazine and inspired by the *Late Turner* exhibition at Tate Britain (2014–15).

Page 44: Another kind of picture!

Page 48: Homage to John Keats.

Page 51: Another favourite painter: Peter Paul Rubens.

Page 55: 'Burd' is a Middle English term for a woman, of unknown derivation but surely cognate with cockney usage 'me bird'!